Robert Rauschenberg
Photographs

Copyright © 1981 by Centre Georges Pompidou and Editions Herscher

All rights reserved under International and Pan-American Copyright Conventions. Published
in the United States by Pantheon Books, a division of Random House, Inc., New York, and
simultaneously in Canada by Random House of Canada Limited, Toronto.

Originally published in France as *Rauschenberg Photographe*
by Centre Georges Pompidou and Editions Herscher

Library of Congress Cataloging in Publication Data

Rauschenberg, Robert, 1925–
  Robert Rauschenberg, photographs.

  1. Photography, Artistic. 2. Rauschenberg,
Robert, 1925–   . I. Title.
TR654.R35   779'.092'4   81–47539
ISBN 0-394-52054-8   AACR2

Manufactured in France
First American Edition

Robert Rauschenberg
Photographs

Pantheon Books

New York

The work of Robert Rauschenberg is full of borrowed images, of images of all kinds – cut out of newspapers and magazines, or simply found; sometimes a more directly personal image is taken from his own photograph album. He was a photographer before becoming a painter. Many years later he returned to photography, and he has now chosen for the first time to display the full range of his work as a photographer.

Followers of his career so far will find themselves in familiar terrain – in the presence of imagery that has made him known as one of the most important and original creative artists of our time. These everyday images, framed in black, set in motion an interplay of shapes in which the human form is integrated to a rigorous yet flamboyant sense of design, pictures in which art and real life coincide. Here is no hiatus. Rauschenberg presents an extract of temporal continuity, everything at once – time compressed, primal energy.

Pontus Hulten

My preoccupation in 1949 with photography was supported by a personal conflict between curiosity and shyness. The camera functioned as a social shield. In 1981 I think of the camera as my permission to walk into every shadow or watch while any light changes. Mine is the need to be where it will always never be the same again; a kind of archaeology in time only, forcing one to see whatever the light or the darkness touches, and care. My concern is to move at a speed within which to act.

Photography is the most direct communication in non-violent contacts.

Robert Rauschenberg
Captiva Island, Florida
11 January 1981

Interview with Robert Rauschenberg
1981 January 9 at Captiva Island, Florida
by Alain Sayag

Why don't you like perfect photography?

If by perfect photography one means maximum of contrast, light and darks and extreme focus, then I don't necessarily desire a perfect photograph. Just like in all other art forms, the object itself is dictating your possibilities. Sometimes you make all the right decisions, and sometimes you can only be either right or very wrong, and sometimes the wrong makes just as interesting a photograph as being right. But you always are dealing in collaboration with the amount of light you have, the scale of the objects, your own physicality – like your size and the distance between you and the ideal photograph – and everything is moving. So I am more or less choked when I get something that appears to be technically a good photograph because it is not necessarily my intention. One gets as much information as a witness of activity from a fleeting glance, like a quick look, sometimes in motion, as one does staring at the subject. Because even if you remain stationary your mind wanders, and it's that kind of activity that I would like to get into the photograph – a confirmation of the fact that everything is moving.

Then perfect photography is only a technique, or do you try in all your work to go further than the technique?

If you always have a perfect negative you will not have any experience in the darkroom except fabrication and I consider the time in the darkroom a very special kind of time that can't be clocked. When I am in the darkroom I don't know whether I have been there for ten minutes or six hours. It's one of the only places where time only exists from accomplishment to accomplishment, because there is no other form of reference in the darkroom. You can't bring the television and the door should be locked, so it's a kind of cloister where you are performing an operation that takes time. The most important part of the medium is time, but you actually have to sacrifice the outside world time in order to measure the darkroom time.

Your photographs are all full frame. Do you ever crop your images?

I don't crop. Photography is like diamond cutting. If you miss you miss. There is no difference with painting. If you don't cut you have to accept the whole image. You wait until life is in the frame, then you have the permission to click. I like the adventure of waiting until the whole frame is full.

You don't miss very often, from looking at the contact sheets.

It's because I wait, I wait until it's there again. Whatever is there is a truth, but a truth you have to believe in. What you see in front of you is a fact. You click when you believe it's the truth. The information is waiting to become in essence a concentration, concentrated so clearly that it can be projected back into real life, into your recognition. It could be any size.

You said time spent in the darkroom is a special kind of time that can't be clocked. What makes it special?

It's your final contact with an experience that you had out-side the darkroom. It's sort of your contract with that experience. Sometimes I have taken photographs and just felt so excited that I could barely hold the camera steady, and the photo was boring. So it's the final contract, verification of the authenticness, the truthness that has begun when you saw an image and decided to photograph.

When I look through the contact sheets there is not a lot of difference among them. Are your selections made only on the basis of size and quality and the final image?

Right, but if there is inconsistency, then I re-evaluate the aesthetic of how important is the technical. Actually, with the new cameras, it is very difficult to make too many mistakes. The technology built into the camera insists that you do things right whether you want to or not. It would almost take a genius to bypass the electronics that are forced onto the camera and therefore the art. Perfection is static, and a flow continues the current. So perfection is not one of the goals because it's a dead end.

Does that mean that perfection is death and instead, you want to recreate at least a sensation?

The eye that looks for perfection is the one that is anticipating a controlled retirement (no matter what the age). So with the photo. The photo can insist on reviewing moments that were unseen, or not know they were seen but passed in viewing. John Cage said (I don't know if they were his own remarks or Zen) his goal was not to get somewhere, he just wanted to enjoy the trip. That's the quality I want in all of my work, that a specific goal or accomplishment would be allied to the fact. I noticed a long time age, when I went to a strange country, that I had the best time and the greatest experiences when I thought I was lost, because when you are lost you look so much harder.

What are the differences between the image you find and the image you make? Is there any difference in your mind?

No, actually taking the photo accomplishes several things. One, it forces me to be in direct contact, intimately, unprotected, in an ambiguous outside world and therefore improve my sight. Also, it gives me a stockpile of both experiences and literal images to draw on for other works. So it's the experience of taking the photograph that keeps my mind open to unprogrammed images, uncontrolled, and then permits me to handle them rawly or allow them to be digested in a cacophony of other specifics.

For a long time you didn't include many of your own images in your work. Why?

Until recently I have used my own photo imagery in paintings, lithographs and engravings only occasionally. I designed a dance set for Trisha Brown and Co. that required several hundred unique photographs. In order for me to edit and select that many images required me to take approximately a thousand new photographs in a short period of time, and I became addicted again. It has heightened my desire to look. The constant survey of changing light and shadows sharpens all of the awarenesses necessary not only to make photographs but functions as fertilizer to promote growth and change in any artistic project. Henri Cartier-Bresson said shyly that he only used his camera as an excuse to see the world.

Was it in this spirit that you made the photographic trip along the East Coast last fall, or was that something you wanted to do long ago?

It was several circumstances. One, I had bought an antique car, a 1936 Phaeton Ford. It was in the north and I had to move it to the south. And knowing about our Paris show I wanted to have as full a pallette of choices to select works from for the exhibition as possible, so I spent nearly a month traveling from Long Island to Captiva Island. Most days Terry Van Brunt, my work assistant, and I didn't travel more than forty miles. The car being open afforded me maximum visibility. One nevertheless can't see in all the alleys and local cracks. Being on foot was the natural alternative. For so many years speed was essential. Jet from one place to another and you don't have the trip. There is no in between, merely one urban airport and another urban airport. Earlier I took a trip with Terry when he bought a 1940 Chevrolet. That was a three-week trip through the Midwest. It felt aesthetically healthy to do that. I confronted myself and a route-bound public newly, observing and resisting and re-evaluating my regional prejudices, and saw for the first time all of the changes and similarities that exist. I have not done the West Coast yet, but this is almost akin to the original idea that made me give up photography when I was studying with Albers. I was serious enough or dedicated enough to know that I could not have at that point two primary professions. My project for continuing, if I was going to be a photographer, at that time was to photograph the entire U.S.A., inch by inch. I was serious and thought 'If I start I will have to finish it, so maybe I'll stay with painting only.' I had everything to learn in either or both, but now I find they are the same thing. My work has always been journalistic, even the most abstract paintings, the most non-image works acquire a presence due to a lack of literal reference and in some cases the aggressive absence of internal information. The all-white paintings were active because an image of light and shadow was always changing. It's your light and your shadow.

I am always afraid of explaining what I am doing, because my mind works so perversely. If I know why I am doing something it immediately goes to another channel and I try not to do that anymore. So in any interview there is a possibility that I have to leave the interview and change my entire life. I think I'll stop now and let the works answer the questions. Too much information is an obstacle to seeing. My works are created to be seen.

1949 - 1965

1

2

3

4

6

7

8

9

10

11

12

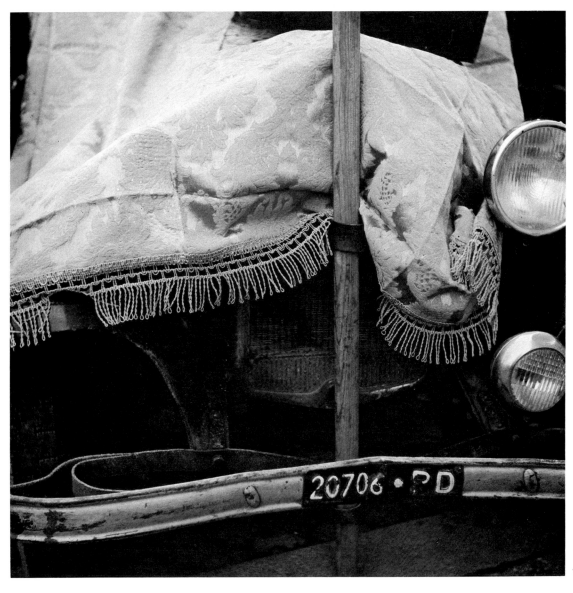

13

14

16

17

20

21

22

23

24

25

26

28

1979 - 1980

29

33

34

35

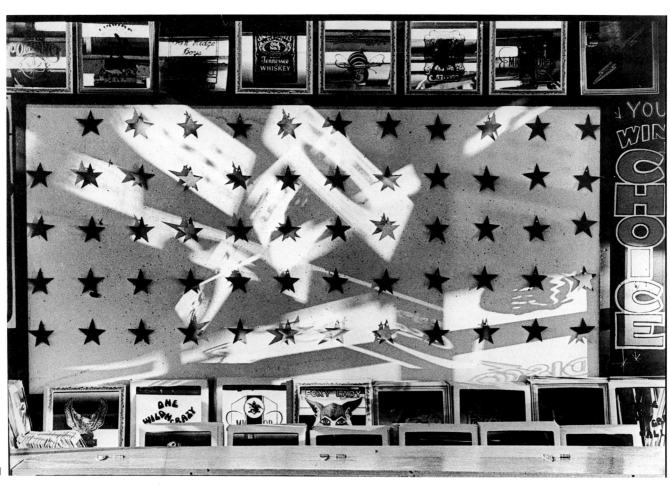

41

42

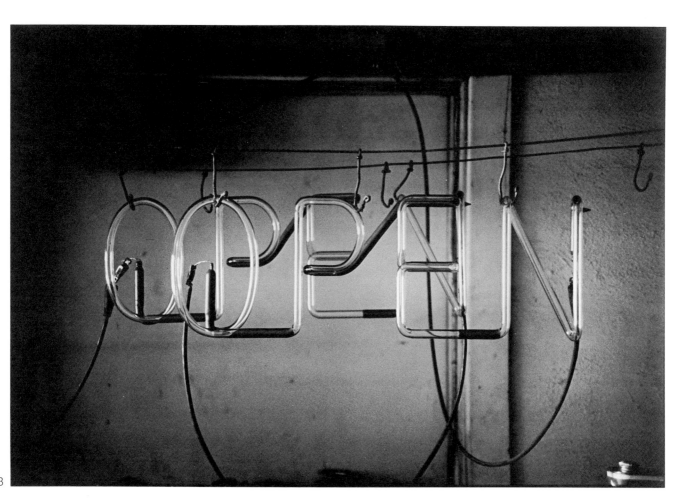

43

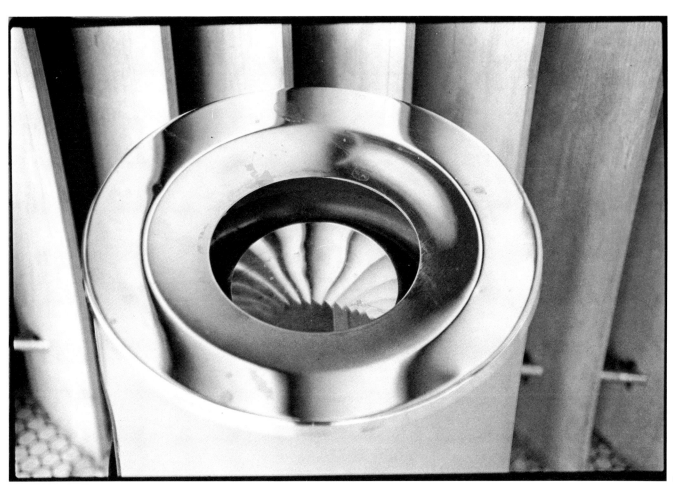

44

46

47

48

49

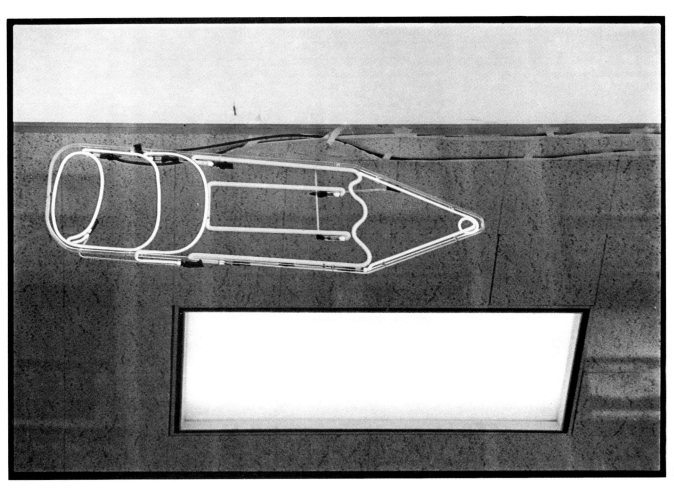

50

52

53

54

57

58

59

67

71

72

74

75

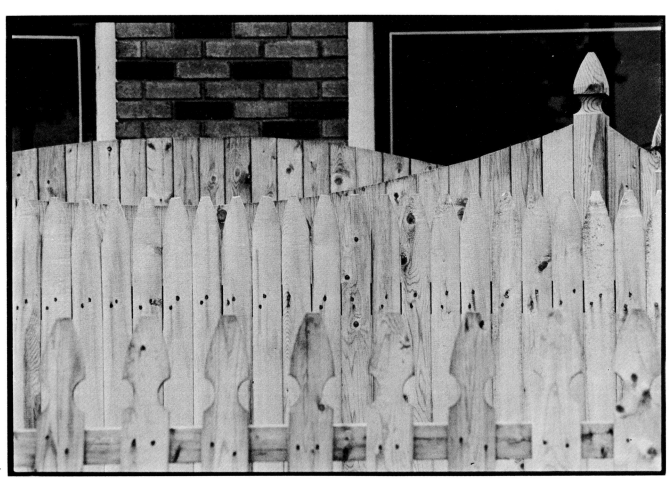

77

78

79

80

82

83

84

86

88

89

90

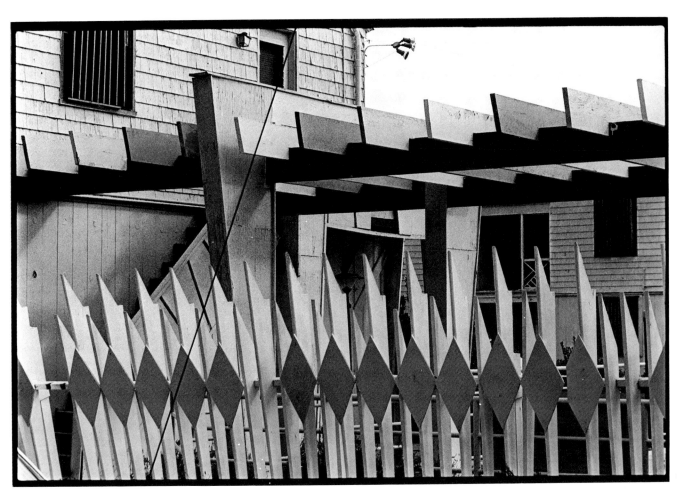

93

94

96

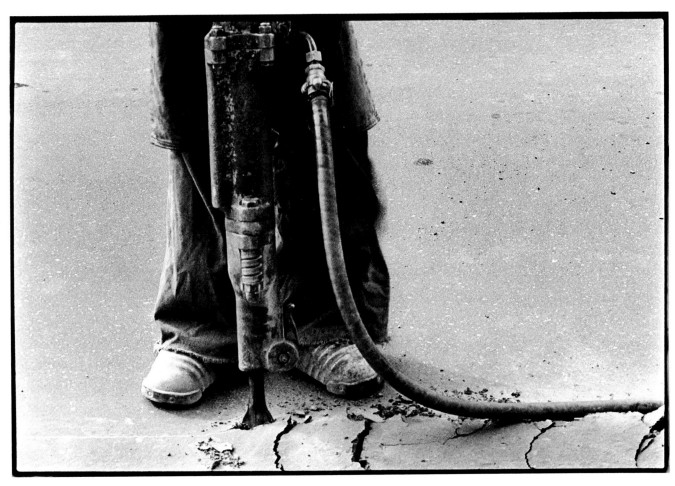

101

102

103

107

108

110

111

116

117

119

120

Captions

Period 1949-1965

1. Quiet House - Black Mountain, 1949
2. Sue + Janet - Outer Island Conn., 1949
3. Ceiling + Light bulb, 1950
4. Susan - Central Park N.Y.C., 1950 (II)
5. Susan - Central Park N.Y.C., 1950 (I)
6. Susan N.Y.C., 1950 (III)
7. Staten Island beach, 1950
8. Cy - Black Mountain, 1951
9. Merce, 1952
10. Charleston Street, 1952
11. Rome Flea Market, 1952 (I)
12. Rome Flea Market, 1952 (III)
13. Rome Flea Market, 1952 (V)
14. Rome Flea Market, 1952 (II)
15. Rome Wall, 1952
16-17. Series of 5 (V) Rome - Cy + Spanish steps, 1952
18. Palermo - Vendors on the sea, 1952
19. Venice Canal, 1952
20. Cy + relics - Rome, 1952
21. Tangier Street, 1952 (II)
22. Tangier Street, 1952 (I)
23. Tangier House, 1952 (I)
24. Laundry N.Y.C., 1955
25. Norman's place, 1955
26. Jasper - Studio N.Y.C., 1955
27. Jasper + Lois - Edisto, S.C., 1962
28. Oracle - Broadway studio, 1965

Period 1979-1980

29. Fort Myers, Florida
30. Fort Myers, Florida
31. Fort Myers, Florida
32. Fort Myers, Florida
33. Fort Myers, Florida
34. Fort Myers, Florida
35. Fort Myers, Florida
36. Fort Myers, Florida
37. Fort Myers, Florida
38. Fort Myers, Florida
39. Fort Myers, Florida
40. Miami, Florida
41. Fort Myers, Florida
42. Fort Myers, Florida
43. Fort Myers, Florida
44. Concorde Lounge, Paris
45. Captiva Island, Florida
46. Cozumel, Yucatan
47. N.Y.C., East Side
48. Fort Myers, Florida
49. N.Y.C., Midtown
50. N.Y.C., Midtown
51. Cozumel, Yucatan
52. N.Y.C., Midtown
53. N.Y.C., Midtown
54. N.Y.C., Midtown
55. N.Y.C., Midtown

The montages on pages 4, 6, 8, 11 and 143 have been created by Robert Rauschenberg especially for this publication, in January 1981.

Acknowledgments

This book could never have been published without the help of Robert Rauschenberg and Mrs Illeana Sonnabend, to whom we offer our thanks. We would also like to express our gratitude to all those who have helped in any way: Antonio Homem (Sonnabend Gallery) and Emil Fray, Larry Massing, Bradley Fray, Todd Harvey, Terry Van Brunt, Eric Holt, assistants at Untitled Press, Captiva Island, Florida.